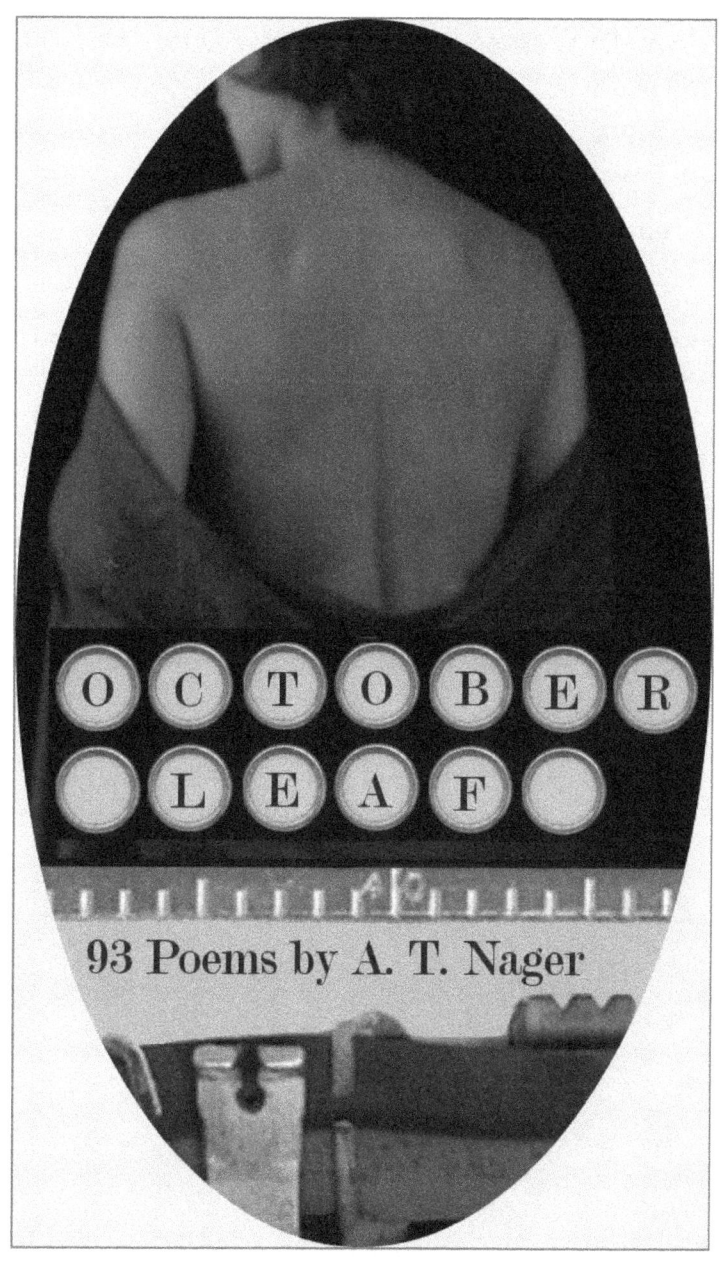

Clocktower Books, San Diego

October Leaf: 93 Poems by A. T. Nager © 2017 by Jean-Thomas Cullen. All Rights Reserved.

These poems are reproduced from the author's collections previously published as Postcards to My Soul and Cymbalist Poems. The latter anthology was published in conjunction with the author's age 27 novel On Saint Ronan Street written while he was a U.S. Army soldier stationed in Europe.

The poems in this collection are the personal intellectual property of Jean-Thomas Cullen, whose rights are registered with U.S. Library of Congress Copyright Office.

Contact:

editorial@clocktowerbooks.com.
Clocktower Books
P.O. Box 600973
Grantville Station
San Diego, CA 92160-0973

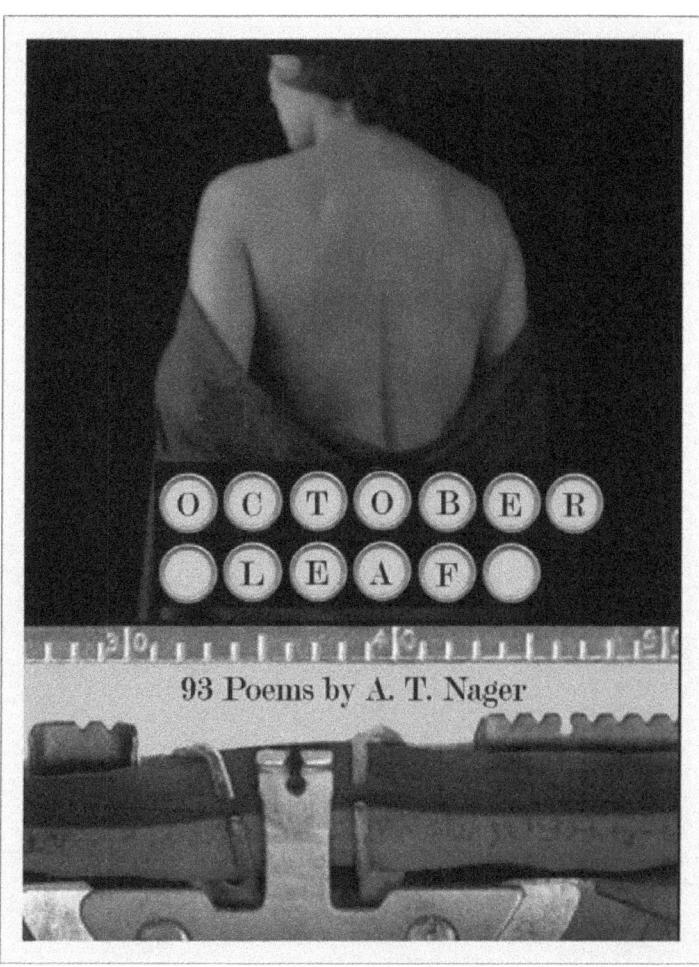

CONTENTS

@@@ Autumn Poems 9
1. OCTOBER LEAF 10
2. COLDFALL 12
3. RAIN (Haiku Chain) 13
4. YOUR EYES (ENNUI) 14
5. AUTUMN TREES 15
6. LITTLE POLAND 16
7. AUTUMN RIVER 18
8. WISH 20
9. SEPTEMBER AFTERNOON 21

@@@ Found 23
10. UMBRELLAS/REFLECTIONS 24
11. MY NAME IS 25
12. TIME-SUN-BOAT 26
13. GREEN WORLD 27
14. AMBER/COFFEE 28
15. BARBARA BELLE 29
16. SHARE 30
17. CAN'T GET ENOUGH 31
18. MY LOVE IS FRIDAY 32
19. PRECIOUS WORDS 33
20. FUN WHILE, FUTILE 34

@@@ College Town 35
21. KING FEVER 36
22. MIRROR TREE/EARTH 37
23. ZEN 38

@@@ Art 39
24. HAIKU (FAN) 40
25. INTERPLAY 41
26. EUROPEAN VILLAGE 42
27. SEES ITSELF 43
28. OFFICE MUSIC 44
29. COMPOSITION I 45
30. JAZZ TRUMPETER 46
31. REDISCOVERIES 47
32. SUN WORSHIP/empire 48
33. AFFIRMATION 49
34. THE WORLD NOT RIGHT 51
35. LAVENDER EXPRESS 53
36. PEAR PICKING SEASON 54
37. FOR COMPANIE 55
38. SPRING FEVER 56
39. COURTLY LOVE 57
40. NOCTURNE 58

@@@ Lost 59
41. WHERE HAVE MY DREAMS GONE? 60
42. BACK STREET BLUES 61
43. LONELY 62
44. I THOUGHT SLEEPING 63
45. NEVER TOLD YOU 64
46. RAIN, TRAFFIC, OPEN WINDOW 65

47.	I LOVE YOU MORE THAN I DON'T	66
48.	IMP	71
49.	LOST LOVE, BLUE EYES	72
50.	BARGAIN	73
51.	GOODBYE	74
52.	LOST LOVE	75
53.	ISLAND STORY	76
54.	SEAMAN'S FAREWELL	77
55.	PIANO	79
56.	SMASHED FLOWERS	80
57.	SINGLES BAR	81
58.	CAFE MACHO 1	82
59.	CAFE MACHO 2	83
60.	BIRTHDAY	85
61.	HOMAGE TO A NUDE	86
62.	MOTH	87

@@@ Astronomies 89

63.	PART OF ME	90
64.	IMPRESSIONISM	91
65.	RATTLING (P)AGES	92
66.	BEAUTIFUL WORDS, MY LOVE	93
67.	SPEAR OF LOVE	94
68.	SOLAR MILK	95
69.	BEACH/FOREVER	96
70.	SENSES, SENSELESS	97
71.	ALIEN	98

@@@ Strange Cities 99

72.	BLACK POEM	100
73.	JUNGLE OPSIS	101
74.	HITCH-HIKE ENDLESS HIGHWAY	102
75.	COLD PASS THROUGH ME	104
76.	FISH POOL WISDOM	109
77.	DISEASE LYRIC	112
78.	YMCA	113
79.	LOST WORLDS	115
80.	MOLLUSKS	118
81.	HYMN TO THE NEW KING	120

@@@ Beautiful Planets 121

82.	SAILOR'S RETURN	122
83.	DOG LOVE	123
84.	HOT DOG VENDOR ON THE BEACH	124
85.	LANDSCAPE, WITH CATS	125
86.	SUMMER THICK AIR	126
87.	SAND AND SUN	127
88.	ANARCHIST DANCES III	128
89.	EVENING	129
90.	WRITING POEMS/INTROSPECTION	130
91.	SEA BED	131
92.	SEA WIND	132
93.	CHILD: COLOPHON	133

@@@ Autumn Poems

1. OCTOBER LEAF

We swept fallen leaves from our door;
leaves we pile each year at Hallow E'en
to treat to trick to delight the kids; but
now it was time for Fall's next chill feast,
giving thanks, turkey day, time to
move on with it all, as time
as wind ever rushes past...

Carolyn picked up one stray fallen leaf
Big and beautiful of dark red blush,
brought it in the house and
laid it on the kitchen counter; she
left it on cold gleaming stone,
marmor crazily polished.

I took the dying leaf and scanned it;
I made its final image in this world
—even as bits of rich dark red
Veiny fading leaf crumbled
on the imaging glass.

Nameless leaf made a fine poem and
When I was done I carried it back
To the kitchen in both hands
for her, for me, for us all to love.

On impulse I raised it to my face,
smelled its frail wings, never expecting: ⇨

Overwhelmed, I inhaled a warm
Fragrance, more life than decay

perfume of a passing woman, a form,
a skirt, a rhythm, music and secret of life,

her smile, her affection, a flirtation
from her heart to mine: instant understanding,
from one life to another —

her beauty, her triumph, and self-assurance,
a warm lingering vegetal ghost, a spirit, a will,
gone before I could catch my breath
but not forgotten;

a life, a truth, her heart still beating
like my own, a personality so strong
it took my voice and breath away.

A memory of who we are, inhalation
A memory while we are,
Her breath shared with mine
Ghost of a lingering moment,
Just as quick forever gone
Eternally lingering equation.

2. COLDFALL

I see
whirling autumn leaves
a turning clock
I see
turning autumn leaves
a whirling clock
Night has fallen
the cold is come
a batting of the
eyes--
not more
a pointing finger in
a window vibrating with frost:
Night is come
the cold has fallen
Nibbling nights with fresh-bread breath
fumbling figures standing in snow
darkness has come
darkness has fallen
the cold

3. RAIN (Haiku Chain)

*

umbrella tilting
in empty rain world swishy
hurry on amber street

*

ah empty rain world!
echoes of my loneliness
wander misty paths

*

blind place of gravel
this rainy day – not seeing,
I wait at the curb

4.　　YOUR EYES (ENNUI)

Your eyes are not on fire;
you sit with lyre in lap
leaning against the window
where evening's sun nectars
deepen, making you drunker;
My eyes chance to caress
your white thighs, soft breast,
your belly all tawny
and honeyed in that opiate light.
Your-eyes are lustrous,
half-closed;
No there is nothing to exchange
more reddish than glances;
And so will you remain,
lazy and reclining between
amber curtains, panes of glass.

5. AUTUMN TREES

It's all here, and I carry you in my soul
Everywhere on earth that I go.
Wind, seasons, stars.

        A humming in the quilted hay lodes.
        The bird, gurgling, softly visits.
        Spring, gently, intrudes.

Trees, leaves, water.

        Autumn trees, their bark armored
                      gray for winter;
        Melting ice, on sandpaper bark
        in me.

6.   LITTLE POLAND

I watch each Saturday in Little Poland
at Allen's Peerless Junk.
It's a ghoulish feast (before lunch)
of licking, lapping flames,
small bodies in the open pit.
They crouch upon a vast
glittering fallen Goliath with
his armor and his baubles -
(You can almost see the giant limbs outstretched,
   a hand upon a sodden chest,
   and think of that
   sausage jumping
   in the bubbling pan at home) -
Chewing little rubber, paper, oilcloth islands
and cardboard cliffs
with rippling, snapping jaws,
but seeming to devour little.   ⇨

Black, smelly smoke whirls upward,
hot within a cold aseptic wind
Etching in summer
inky filth on a humid sky;
In autumn,
dark warmth in cold gray air;
In winter
disappearing into streams of falling snow
that cover the lukewarm scrap heap with
a grayish film;
In spring
Green:
testimony to the new by old things burning.
That's all year round at Allen's Peerless Junk
on Pilsudski Street
near the black old iron railway bridge.
So come, won't you,
come with me, our bellies empty,
and we'll watch the flames this Saturday
(thinking of bubbling kielbasa)
feasting before their week-long fast.

7. AUTUMN RIVER

Swirling roundly, river flow,
by cobbled banks
and marshy shores,
racing like the clouds
in the cold grey wind;
    Standing windblown in the eddies
    at your swollen rim,
    reeds and swamp grass lean,
    beaten by the spray of
    foam boats rolling by;
Running moody, River talk
to fish laid on the banks, and
wild geese darting in the gray…
Under wharves and bridges, 'round
small boats backing as
you roll along; ⇨

Gripping frothy waves with
curling fingers ride
dying leaves, drifting
from the marsh stream in a circle
then into your center stream;
Dark waters, run along,
with your booty on your heaving back,
squawking as you rumble, but faintly
for the noise you make:
    Festive turkeys stolen from the farm,
    bucking boxes from the pier, and
    trees you've bitten off with
    grinding teeth of thunder;
Happy am I, with
my net ashore, and
my dinghy on the wharf, and
my pantry filled for winter feasts:
    Godspeed, Autumn River!

8. WISH

As it always will,
summer rain reminds
of autumn thoughtfulness.
Sudden chill, darkness,
uneasy wind in the leaves,
the unease mere melodrama…
because all is and was as
it was and always will be -
Man, and the Wish to Be.

9. SEPTEMBER AFTERNOON

College Courtyard

(i)

window

Stone
and Leaves

Open
and Wind

(ii)

Gargoyles:

Strange
where they put Faces

@@@ Found

10. UMBRELLAS/REFLECTIONS

umbrellas

in the sunshine

rain drops twinkle

on my toes

when I

look down

I see two people

smiling

in the puddle

11. MY NAME IS

Thank you for being so friendly.
It is cold to deal with technicians.
Let me take off my uniform, girl,
and yours, and let us look deep.
I am the continent-conscious,
The lost on highways, the walker by night.

Who are you?
    Whose companion are you,
And what do you desire?

        My name is
        Who are you?

12. TIME-SUN-BOAT

dust river
in my veins

soft powders falling
through lime-colored windows
crystal snowflakes
marching thickly

tangerine glass
brandy-world shimmers
window sill apples sweetly

heart-throb love time
sweet kiss on an orange cloud
heady liquor love-belly
egg skin soft-warm
drops of peach nectar

sky-ceiling, blue window wall
lemon sea spray
bright sails on a milk sea

dust of soft oil drops
(falling featherly over)
over under down and down
softly sleep me in your arms.

13. GREEN WORLD

We sing
in a green world

walking sun-paths
dappled green

  ships of leaf
    drift gently

      where our echoes
      am happy

        we got on

          there is soft.

14. AMBER/COFFEE

    good
    I'm happy
here is the amber
of smoke and coffee
warmth and laughter
our thighs are one
we almost
need not say the
things that are
making us laugh

hey

15. BARBARA BELLE

she rides in sunshine,
Time she conquers, sun time

She's an Egyptian queen
lost in tapestries of green
on a black mare
who's a nightmare
He carries her over fences
stings her with lances
snares her in trances
She takes her chances
because she's an Egyptian queen
like none you've ever seen

She sings songs from a dusky cave
she longs for a man who's brave
who crosses the light-engreen-crusted hills
with sad eyes warning (here my soul lingers)
and points to the earth
far-flung soul's sweet berth

and the hills have hips
   whips and shapely lips
legs wide open to the sea.

16.　SHARE

Darling
I want to share your dreams
come with me
out of all time & place
   to a sort
         of dark
or at least
sort of vague
       world
 of
   soft
        discordant notes

a piano maybe
        of railroad tracks
French antiquity
        smelling of old iron
but mellow with rain

        and forgottenness.

(yeah, we KNOW, don't we?)
a kind of happy nothing

and I'll love you
      and you'll love me
and maybe just maybe
        we'll learn …
            mellow ….
                …passing.

17. CAN'T GET ENOUGH

can't get enough
I'm havin a ball
can't get enough
she tells him
and he tries again
poor catholic virgin
Holy Roman Priestess
can't see enough
in blinding light.
what does it take
to burn out the stars?
what does it take
to turn a marble statue warm?
O marble goddess
let him be your faun
let him hurt himself on you
but forgive him
if he pulls away
when the fire dies.
what does it take
to make flames
in a marble goddess?

18. MY LOVE IS FRIDAY

my love is Friday
she'll always stay
with me on our sailboat
wherever we may float
        I took her from the sea
        in a week of circling sharks
        cannibals on iron-laden barks
        and we are both free
                are we,
                are we,
                she sings to the sea
        are we,
        are we,
        she sings to me

19. PRECIOUS WORDS

        Love is now the only ink
        that sets my pen flowing.
That I should be marooned on such an island,
        Tentacles rippling in-sea,
        cut off from all but this rock.
My thoughts, long buried in the soil
of fiery, unsubstantial imagination,
then disurned and carried in-Sun dry as Roman humus,
in lumbering barrows, whistled-behind, tramped-behind-
                in heavy boots,
breathed-on by warm sausage breath, stale beer,
now their own cave-kept lantern.
        And you, who I thought never to see again,
        Write me this letter of introduction,
        Postmarked for the island, to read me,
        to caress in me the precious words.

20. FUN WHILE, FUTILE

You're in my mind, and my heart, in my structure,
You're in my eyes, in my blood, in my fingers,
lovely dreamer wearing our thoughts.
I've got you boarded up with driftwood
and salvage from a silk mill.
I've got you shining through my window,
I've got you jumping in my river,
You've got me lying on your leaves,
trying on your clothes,
flying on your Peter Pan-Am.
You've got me, I've got you,
we've got places to go,
things to do, before tomorrow
becomes yesterday.
Let me cruise through your eyes
because I'm young and strong,
I'll bring you news of tomorrow before long.
So stay inside my railway
stay with me in the pumpkin coach.
I'll sit beside you forever,
and tell you what I'll never need to say,
and I'll promise you things you'll never
really need, just to fill your suitcase,
my presence—Sunny Fool, Sunny Fool…

@@@ College Town

21. KING FEVER

The cities are sister-wives of the king.
Harem slaves the conquered foreign ports.
Men are stick figures
sweating over womanly ships.
Everywhere is the king, fucking.

(Renaissance)

22.   MIRROR TREE/EARTH

- - - Spade my loam and be my shady leaves.
I will be your tree and you my earth.

23. ZEN

Our lives are mosaics of emotion.
Together, we spin worry and joy.
The implanted anxieties seek survival;
the past, revival; growing up more difficult.

Every day, new. Discovery is unfamiliar.
Not so boxed, we face at every moment
an infinity of choices. Reject all, and
there remains no guide firm in anything.

Freedom is a harried cross.
Self-imposed. And then the anxiety,
trying not to feel self-pity.
Overloaded. No circuit room left for pity.

Reality is a harsh morning light.
Ago, morning light was harsh reality.
In freedom, also, sharp reversals.
The beat remains steady. We?

--Avoid unnecessary concern for self.

@@@ Art

24. HAIKU (FAN)

Oh, this heat! –Fan: ON
--your petals like spring water,
cool air to inhale!

25. INTERPLAY

Green expanse,
　shimmering glass
　　roof.
Wind there is,
　water runs
　　nowhere.
Glimpses:
　Cherub face
　　vanished in water;
Age-green watery metal fixtures:
Victorian cherub, youth,
green with age, what is this vision?
Trees, over the flat roofs away,
green and young beyond wetness
　in wind.
Cberubs: trumpeting memories,
Nautilus shells filled
　with tomb ash　and yet
　green leaves
　scrubbed and dripping
　in cleansing wind!

26. EUROPEAN VILLAGE

On a table standing in the grass--
Victorian bones of wood clashing with
        spider blades -
Rests the sky rocking softly
  as the ever lightly haze
   brought forth from tremors of vastness
   echoes from an empty hall filled with
  silent wind
  and colors.
Wind
behind my.eyes
fills my forehead with hair
waxes my cheeks
dries my lips
From the village where the people live
the church bell is ringing noon:
Wafting sensations of stew, of sauce, of
meat, unstoppered wine, sense of
  being somewhere else or nowhere
(hunger) but how possibly in this place?
The hay, the hay, Jean Pierre
The tails off the carrots, quick!
Come, children, we shall pray;
Eat, for it is given;
yes, the fields

27. SEES ITSELF

conch of consciousness:
two-edged *
  flitting sea-scissor,
  sword of existence *
  in the dread shallows:
That * instant
(round the wall)
retreat *
And sees itself.

28. OFFICE MUSIC

&
60¢
steno success
open
spring door
Coca Cola
/
skirt
hi,
**(see p.
dominant and.
stocks bru bra
broke the
!
typo'
bond paper
desk calendar
"Coffee with)
open door
Spring
voices
"While I
a fly!
want to close
the door please?

29. COMPOSITION I

on a white wall:
switches, three:
OFF, ON, ON

30. JAZZ TRUMPETER

Jazz Trumpeter at climax of a
particularly demanding solo:
    <u>Heow!</u>
    (lips to the horn,
      puts his lips to the horn)
        <u>Heow!</u>

31. REDISCOVERIES

That
which discovered long ago
smells good, again and again
That which rediscovered
after once found
long ago and with
ooh and aahh
never loses
its power to surprise
again and again
What was once given
is given again
and again,
coming in disguises
or at a different hour,
on a different train maybe,
but this fresh
ever market
again and again,
Morning,
or Spring sunshine
or a new Love,
it feels so good again,
and never lose the
pebble to enchant!

32. SUN WORSHIP/empire

    We worship the Sun.
Even in our architectural criminalities
   is justice, as in the dagger's shining eye.
All light is the light of atoms and stars.
The moon and the knife
share splendor's distance.
The knife is on the Earth's dark side
--stabs but she does not whimper--
and the knife is
    miles, miles from the Sun,
    miles from the Moon.
The Moon is an eerie dream of the Earth head.
The knife is carried by a lunatic messenger,
   who built the pyramids,
     drowsing tortoise herd in the desert.
     In the Sun.
But the Sun also shines
on the archaic sky line of New York.
   The winds there
(the windows are opera glasses)
   sing songs of empire.

33. AFFIRMATION

Welcome, World, with all your vinegar!
Welcome, Reality, triumphant beast!
Welcome, Sunlight, feast of splendor!
After the deep galaxies of my brainself
are done exploding
And the abrupt, calamitous young stars
   finished with their wild music
Welcome, subtle golden sunlight
who sting my narrowed eyes,
and ride the sweet summer wind in the
leaves, green airport of insects!
There is, after all, only one fate,
one destiny, bereft of gods and devils,
free of angels, demons, deaf to prayers,
mysterious to squinting diviners. ⇨

This is my destiny, limited but honored credit,
to take upon my shoulders if I chose --
   and choose I do,
like Bunyan wrapping the ox around his neck.
I want to carry my fate beyond the fence
toward the looming green-black forest
beyond the symphony of my best years.
As the dull black cipher
unfolds into a mighty dream,
so there is, again and again, only morning
to drive the night away: Precise,
rich in changing colors,
vibrant and harmonious guitar,
the well-tuned life.
All things, from here, follow of themselves:
Dawn the night which follows day,
insight the dull cipher,
perfect mnemosyne the splendid here and now!

34. THE WORLD NOT RIGHT

The world was never right,
I guess
In the good old days
the devil was loose
roaming the world
seeking the ruin of souls
one awoke at night
sweating in dread
at the howl of a dog
chained to a fence
at the edge of town
edge of the world
where men have set foot
on the moon
was an alien planet
thought to be a face
made of cheese,
with unknown terrors, tygers,
behind fitful running clouds, ⇨

where today
against the sweet silver moon
runs a gleaming 707
easily surmounting
the dark turquoise sky
We who huddled in caves, cold,
afraid even of warming fire
poured from the sky by our
generous sky father/earth mother,
afraid we were, afraid we are,
still all the old instincts,
still that sweating in the night,
world not right, never right,
poor world, poor us.

35. LAVENDER EXPRESS

Lavender express, hear me in your dignity:
I abuse time, am buffeted (and your shoulder
   is hard as the next) but none my fault.
Take then my bitter tendrils, my roots, shoots,
my herbal corona, unbury me from the wires;
I have stopped, and am ready to start over.

36. PEAR PICKING SEASON

(fragment)

at random, a luxury:
hands in the fence, shaking
clustered leaves, gnarly twigs
as glistening sticky
globes dangle
then drop
plop plop
one by one.

37. FOR COMPANIE

Fingers smelling of wood swarths,
like bacon from the fireplace,
She kept me Companie;
In the room in the cottage,
in that roome by the lake,
she kept me Companie;
Round-breasted, rumpled white sweater
  stuck with bits of autumn leaf,
  alive with borrowed fire colors*
    (* and we catalog the burning of
    fires, and homeliest
    is wood burning in fire places,
    food in iron places,
    bacon and chestnuts, wood
    and auburn hair, such a girl was she)
Her hair, her sweater, warm, emanent
with fragrance of fresh leaf
and common burning wood: Wine
from Madeira, Virginian tabacos,
were shipt to us,
for Companie!

38. SPRING FEVER

(fragment)

Softly visits the gurgle-bird,
spring gently presses,
 heartbeats quicken in
 the quilted hay-yield,
Spring gently presses.

39. COURTLY LOVE

The words are spoken from our fingertips:
    Love, you are best to be with.

You are swift in piercing, hunter--
    my heart seeks you everywhere.

    Pictures, portraits,
    lutes, and pergaments;
White stag bleeding on the rocks;
Two lances broken in his side.

40. NOCTURNE

Your wind, my empty friend,
come to fill my open hands--
the night is his bellyful purse,
come to clatter pennies on my knuckles.
The mountains in the city have neon.
A trumpet is still, I know, because
because of his hand, to her breast,
and her hand, rising to caress.
An empty coat's the wind's tent,
air in trumpet's wet with osculations,
he signed his name and
folded the canvas away.
Somewhere, I think, butterflies
   and children.
Gomez saw and heard the elevation.
Eddie cried and sang and drank
   into his radio.
I am a stranger here
but these streets treat me
as if I'd never been away.

Lost

41. WHERE HAVE MY DREAMS GONE?

where have my dreams gone?
dreams of time immemorial
to which I was not chained
but swimming in colored glass
I hear the sigh of sound
filling an hourglass
waiting for silence
to tell me it's over
memory comes in a cloud of pain
filling my future empty
with transparent shade pictures
that I know will never be
oh someone tell me it's not so
and you all come around
with your comforting advice
but your dreams aren't even mine
for a while there's a girl
we share the same dreams
but then we cross through each other
and walk along shadow paths, silent
still I keep seeing new mornings
forgetting the night ahead
walls that seem solid
until I walk relentlessly through
give me no promises
to stop the earth turning round
just share my time a while
I'll keep my shoes by the door.

42. BACK STREET BLUES

I know a man on Back Street
who keeps a shop for broken dolls
and he loves to make them
of paper mache
and he loves to keep them
when they break

no one ever hears him speak
stays in his shop all week
with his armless dolls
all hanging on the walls
Poor little man he whispers
like he had no voice

but at night I can't sleep
I hear him weep
I hear him in the attic room
waiting for the dream coach
to come and take the brideless groom
to some dollhouse church
where dreams of love come true

43. LONELY

Sometimes I think
when you can't be
lonely with your friends

it's better to be lonely
by yourself

than to be lonely
among strangers.

44. I THOUGHT SLEEPING

I thought
sleeping with you
would be excusable

I thought I saw a woman
behind the paint on your face
your expensive smell & kept coats
and silly hostile giggles
of the lost & isolation ego trip
(yes in bed your body
        was very soft & very white
        Your cunt made a hot
        tugging tube
        around my
            sliding penis;
        The soft   warmth of your
        thighs pres   sed against my
          legs on   both sides
        You moaned and pulled
        at me with   your arms)
I saw in your eyes and empty simperings
high walls topped with bars
and the bars meshed with
barbed wire
        the only thing the wall stopped
        I think was the gray rain sky
        the wet scudding clouds (which
        bled black on the wall in passing)
        because I think
        the people they gave up
        already and forgot who they
        were and what it was that
        they were supposed to be   doing
            other than   playing cards
or hanging clothes or sitting
unemployed in the plaza of
the   concrete/iron slum.
    (I CAME---
      a sick feeling---
      and cried for escape.

45. NEVER TOLD YOU

Brown-eyed girl, I love you
and I never said a word.
Behind the shadows of my skin
I hid a sleeping flower bud
and when it would not open
I hid it from myself and
there it remains, reminding me
of you sometimes, of you,
brown-eyed girl.

46. RAIN, TRAFFIC, OPEN WINDOW

afterthoughts, the   aftertaste
bares my champagne
   to the   empty apartment.
rain, traffic, open window.

-and you   on some night curb-
-a prism for your thoughts-
a tear drop, a sip of my   champagne.

47. I LOVE YOU MORE THAN I DON'T

I won't know why but lately it seems
the tears are flowing easy, and life
has been so full of uncertainty.
I often think of leaving you,
but I stay another week anyway,
waiting for the puzzle to fall in place.
But the time turns too slow
and my time is so short
and winter is turning into spring.
I want to fly with you,
but I'm afraid we have tickets
to a different plane, I don't know yet,
and you don't either, and
the weeks that pass
might still make our tears
flow down a single cheek.
I also want to fly away from you,
but you've become so much a part of me,
and the truth is just another lie,
so why not take destiny in hand,
and risk the ups and downs another day.
You've brought me back to life it's true,
you've brought me love and affection,
you've shared my laughter and tears,
you took me from a bad track
and put your needle in my veins,
I always come back for more... ⇨

When I'm away I can't recall your name
because your face is buried in my heart.
Your voice tells me one thing,
but your arms tell another story.
          It seems the world is moving the way I want
          because I've left the stars alone
      And yet I cry when I can't recall my name.
      And I weep when I see the things I've become
      And I laugh when I hear the songs of misery
      I am hard on myself and hard on you
      because I see the day when a single word
      will seem completely true.
      Oh come all ye good doctors
      say how it's supposed to be
      but I smile when I'm full
      and I cry when I'm empty.
      In the end maybe
      the highway will be my faithful dog
      we on a leash to each other
      We build each other little bridges, baby,
      but I have so much traffic to you
      and the river never changes course.
      I find it hard to live for just today
      because I've been drifting so long
      and I want to let down a new sail,
      (Don't) take a sunny day to sail away with me
      and vanish in the morning,
      don't leave me oarless on the open sea.
      Sometimes everything seems ok
      and sometimes I feel like such a fool
      I don't have the strength to say goodbye
      I wonder if I have the strength to stay. ⇨

>   You're so concerned about your emptiness
> lately it seems that's what you're full of.
>   But when I offer to fill your heart
>   You tell me you don't care.
>   and I feel so stabbed. You talk about love,
>   But you don't really care.
>   You've been trying hard, You talk
>   about beauty, but you're full of fear,
>   you're full of sorrow for your sad state,
>   your sorrow is your only meaning
>   when you cry like that.
> You're running from me, baby,
> but I also see you running from yourself.
> You blame me for the sorrows,
> but I also suffer, I didn't make the world,
> and what does it matter
> if you cry when you're alone,
> when we're together that is in the past.
> Your strength is fantasy,
> fantasy my weakness.
> So when you have your visions
> you don't even see me
> holding you with these tender arms
> your eyes are in the future
> your eyes are in the distance
> you dream dreams of childhood
> childhood you think as it was
> you dream of the farthest islands
> your thoughts run faster
> than the far-flying endless telephone lines.
> Oh I know I shouldn't talk
> I've had even longer to be messed up.   ⇨

        I have walked through an inferno
        my mind gasping like a fish on sand
        strangers have held my head
        while I puked in my despair.
        But that religion is gone
        I mailed the cross away,
        I tore up the list of sacred words
        I threw out the honor roll of saints,
        and I've been trying so hard
        to make my stand.
        You say I see no beauty,
        you're wrong, only I see through the illusion
        of skin-deep beauty.
        I am the meaning of my words
        I am very careful in my choice.
        though somehow I always seem to turn out wrong.
I told you I love you,
and as your eyes closed gray with meaning,
the wind blew the frozen letters away.
Quicksilver shimmering, touch it and it contracts.
        It's true you've tried to bring love
        but invitations to an empty house bring only regret.
You feel afraid of love returned,
you feel evil in the exchange,
you walk in your cathedral
with the mud of human feelings on your feet.
If I were dreaming, and if I saw in you an angel,
yes, I guess, I could feel wrong,
knowing what I know, feeling as I feel.
But I see you only as a person,
with only the glow of true affection,
and I can only resent it   ⇨

when you spit your angel shit at me.
But having said these things I am tired again
soon you'll have alittle time for me again
Oh baby how wrongly I accused you
When I thought those things of you,
when I doubted your words,
those times when I hated you.
Now, even though you hurt me,
even though you hurt me,
even while you hold and kiss me,
I love you more than I don't.
I have faith in my survival –
something a falling angel doesn't.
In the end all things will be equal
the good times, the bad, will fall away.
I'm just waiting for the revelations
as they come, I'll try real hard to be good,
I'll really try to remember my medicines,
I'll wait morning after morning
and pray each night to be better.

48. IMP

Every time you say you love me
I watch your eyes turn distant
Every time you hold me
I feel emptiness between your arms
Baby I'm tired of kissing the heels
of dreams revealed to little girls
I am Jesus and have my dreams to run from
Mickey Mouse has nothing over you.
You are the queen of lonely aces
You never say no, you never say yes
You only smile until they touch you
Then you bite, then you run, howling.
Let's trip to your kingdom
Let's enjoy this tyranny
Your whips are made of glances
Your chains are made of smiles
And all I can do is run away
YesyesI can only leave.

49. LOST LOVE, BLUE EYES

Last space ship in, the space age is over.
It was too far to America, and we have
rediscovered god in the unfathomable
sea where we have finally realized the
meaning of ∞.
    Dear Faith, dawn still creeps every aging day
    with pink fingers through the green
    and dew beyond my window - -
    as it always has.
And lost love as surely as dawn
turns into dry summer day.   She
went away. I passed from her mind
like a heavy stone. Adolescent fantasy?
Read on. It's all in the stones, like
the Mountain's face. Critique, like
theology and like ∞, is brushed aside
by pink fingers dripping with dew.
I have rediscovered Ω∞Ω. I tear from
a stoned heart this thought: fly far,
my love, my dear sweet friend
    of a past year,
    of a shared dream,
my beloved companion. Fly far,
let many dewy dawns rise out of
your blond hair. May those marvelous
blue eyes of yours often rise from
shadow into sunlight, your pupils
contract in twin clear blue flashes.
You take with you a piece of my heart,
far as long as you remember me.
And I, you. Faith is my prayer,
love my hawk-borne gift. Far, far,
fly, memory, swift but homeless thought!

50. BARGAIN

Oh if I could have you back
I'd bargain all my ambitions
and conquests against your
soft mind-and-body empathy
beside me in my car.

When I die I think I'll scream
and make a last failing grasp
toward all the selves I could have been.

Yet they, like you, never were –
and if they might have been,
Time, time inexorable
vanishes as unused codes
of past and could alike.

Day is the choice,
dusk the sentence,
night its execution.

I swear to you now,
before these witnesses —
Yearning, Melancholy, deep
Volcanic Grief, and also
a Love shamed by meaningless scribbles
and acts transformed into their own atrophy —
I would give all other futures
If I could only have you back again.

51. GOODBYE

when I said good-bye to this girl, now,
somewhere, deep inside me, was a rumbling I know tomorrow or
sometime soon will erupt in me - - no Krakatoa, but reiteration...

for dreams, the Indian Summer wind pushes around the corners
under the dark moonlit gables where leaves drive shadows once only, each,
over concrete pores.

the up, the down of the dry branches,
is the echo of my welled tears.
oh, another, mother, again,
and I am mute to bring back with spells
the yesterdays enchantment shrove.

my poor mind, little ship, against all nothingness,
when I am alone, the spectres gain flesh and well up in words,
like images from a tarny well.mother, father, best friend, love less however,
for there and there only can we say good-bye, hello, good-bye, only in
love, most talked-about and supernal of all the emotions...

the past, farther than distance, gone, never was,
I too, and cry for all the was and all the won't be.

52. LOST LOVE

                      (icy moment)
Ruthlessness has no cuttinger edge
   than a love reconspired alone
   and cut from itself
   in the ice
Of rediscovered solitude.

53. ISLAND STORY

The dull oak by its trembling leaves
dreams the acorns' bounding gonadity.
Drunk on sunlight, we climb the mast.
We scan, tattered, for passing virgins.
The horizon, however, has shrunk;
all is but a dream, a prayer,
the reenactment is a resignation.
A strong, narrow-eyed youth climbed the oak.
He saw the ship and sailed.
Later as a young man he fell captive to love
   in a Berber queendom. A vengeant king
soon came and slew the youth.
Ever after, a quiet man with troubled eyes
   paces the island's tropic rim.
   With binoculars he scans the mainland.
The youth's grave is but
   a shallow plot of turned earth
   and the leaves shake, rattling, over it,
   the man visits it often.
The king's spear lies gross and green
in the ocean rim.
Sea horses dance in the boiling waters,
   conches sleep on the deep highways;
No virgin waves in the misty distance.

54. SEAMAN'S FAREWELL

Men recently emerged from the sea
tend to sunshine, vanilla, and soft company
Men who have swum ashore
like to head home in late afternoon
carrying striped bags, ice cream cones.
Men
leaving their armor, their halberds,
pitards in steaming salty sand,
like to dry themselves before the screen doors
of shops dry and scoured inside
    like the gleaming chestnut shell
    redolent chic cork, leather, polished driftwood. ⇨

But come time, they back against the sea,
arms spread to the stone cliffs.
Silently, reluctantly, they take their armor
   from the sand,
   wrap themselves in drying cords
   and belts
   of moss-green sea weed,
   pick up lheir king crab shells and
   barnacle-and-scallop crusted tridents,
     and walk slowly
      into the deepening tide.
When cars are parked and naked knees cooling
         under kitchen tables,
   The sun drifts to rest
   among tangled trees.
A buoy abandoned on a sand bar
comes to life with the tide.
The waves of the sea are briefly bowls to the sky.
The closing of the waves
Over the last wave of a limp hand
is the merciful end to a lingering goodbye.

55. PIANO

My thoughts played piano
long and softly from your eyes.
I could have put your apples in a jar
but there were places to stay
(while you chafed to go)
and you left
(you said you would)
me in poetic triumph

56. SMASHED FLOWERS

(timeless moment)

The hearth is visible.
You, fine girl, broke the flowers
which became running greyhounds
at the wetted fireplace.

57. SINGLES BAR

Are you going early, and alone?
<u>Stay</u>. We
  are the driftwood of
  conversation, fragments of
  ambitions, broken halves,
  the late lamp. In this
  our deep and distant eyes
  glanced to agree.
<u>Stay</u>. My voice
  is inaudible, but my eyes
Are screaming.

58. CAFE MACHO 1

Man of great deeds, o violent life!
He sees his story as one of drink and smoke:
precipitous, with red nights and lightning days;
painful encounters with careless or impulsive women;
friends with guns - he is of battlements,
   sailing ships, and cannonades!
Women (when they see him lingering
        with his Marlboro
        over an expensive drink)
think: there
sits a gentle and unsuccessful man.

59. CAFE MACHO 2

Your string has fallen,
pharaonic dancing girl,
I see your tan skin
in the flute music;
in the liquor,
the dusky lounge,
the airconditioned dance place
with women to pick from,
pastiche of loves
that might have been
were it not for…
What tender celebration
if you were you
and I were I
but here we are all
the should be,
the would be, and may be…   ⇨

She walks out to accept this dance,
her eyes are black and fierce,
her beauty is terrible, ringing,
like an army with banners flying.
She deigns to accept this embrace
from the ninety-ninth shadow
of the man she gave her soul.
O essential grace,
the jazz of your dry skin
is beige and angled in motions.
You evoke, essential grace,
music; it was I, once,
who took your soul.
For the space of a dance,
the embrace of a trance,
quite by chance,
we relive my long ago night
and some evening of yours
before you had your hair cut and styled,
when you possessed your youngest beauty.
Your smile is a white feather
floating in my air-conditioned eyeballs.
Your tan and tennis face
is full of invitations,
reasons, address cards.

60. BIRTHDAY

(fragment)

I begin to feel
measureless loss of youth -
itself
abdication from jeweled childhood.

61. HOMAGE TO A NUDE

O Cheek and Smile,
ye buttock moon,
orchestra of fingers,
long legs, and pink belly,
pear breasts with stem nipples,
center fold, still life,
still I think it is the
source of light--
your smile.

62. MOTH

You annoyance,
brief,
because after a moment's anger
I reflect on the justice
    of your presumption,
      the dignity of your proclamation,
as you enter your last wild dance,
dervish,
moments before you die thrashing
in the cauldron of desire
around the light bulb.

Astronomies

63. PART OF ME

part of me is very old
part of me is very young

together
they tear me in half.

64. IMPRESSIONISM

worlds of measured time
imploding slowly from
all directions in ka
leidoscope
colors around all
corners and quietly

disappear in ego-hole

65. RATTLING (P)AGES

Sometimes I look up
from my droning text

look deep among the trees

idly flip rattling pages back

and bend my head again
merge into passing ages

[Alt title: History Reader]

66. BEAUTIFUL WORDS, MY LOVE

The words are beautiful, my love,
spoken from our fingertips.
you are so good to be with.

Marble of Greece, red of Carthage,
Shubiluliuma, Hatshepsut,
Antony, Cleopatra,
Romeo, Juliet,
Yellow, Cathay, Indigo, Brasilia
Hymen, Hymen, Hymenaiee

Blue sea
you drown our secret words

Sun, shine, sun shine,
take our hearts to the cliffs

Two lances broken in his side
A thousand deaths in her belly.

67. SPEAR OF LOVE

…You are swift in piercing, Love;
my heart seeks you out…

(fragment)

68. SOLAR MILK

Dear heart in my breast,
locus of half my sickness,
my brain the other aching half,
how I infect myself
with this muddled desire!
Such distraction my malady,
such malady my distraction,
toxic distillation scouring the beds
of my blood's river, the musseled
beaches of my thoughts' ocean!

My own disposition
is the poison of my life.
The world is me
I abhor the world, and
thereby abhor myself.

Come, blessed contradiction,
numb the quadrilles of my prison.
Come, come, dear berries of day,
oozing the sweet sun's milk,
rub away the noxious sleep around my eyes!

Aye, this fevered throe
shakes my head in yes's and no's,
makes the giving hand a fist,
the poet's tongue a sour, cringing twist,
and love's death's soliloquy a prolog
                      to the golden hours.

69. BEACH/FOREVER

It has always bothered me
        vaguely
that in this sea of dreams
my dreamship should
choose to run aground
        softly
on the open armed trees…
darkness dancing with light;
bowers of spring blossoms…
blends of grassy green and blue sky…
bosom of turned black earth puddings…
        and
HOUSE   cornering on life and death.
(maybe I should run;
for my small FOREVER.)

70. SENSES, SENSELESS

do you smell the roses, the moss, the grass, and bath steam?
the evening, the sunlight, the trees growing in the windows?
the faint cigarette smoke, the blue haze of gasoline?
do you feel the urge to write,
the passion fro a close and silent friend?
do you thrive on time and time alone,
and do you offer hot green summery solitude?
a meadow? a flight of bees, a flutter of wings?
have you a table whose napkins are windscattered,
a glass tinkling with ice and fountains of pinprick soda?
careless legs on a chipped white chair, sandals,
muscles and soft skin, roundness of pliant
flesh trim and ever-undulant with quick unpretending motions?
have you a free day, a cigarette, a light, a night to spare,
a little time to delay your promises to yourself?

71. ALIEN

Velvet currents, silver bubbles
   in the deep
     below an amber water sky...
!To stand on a pearl dust planet
A million miles below a certain
              bobbing bow...
Alone
Among a billion fleeting shapes,
   Alien,-
    (darting silver daggers
      gaping rusty discs
        hacksaw wings...)
   Here is death a quiet dream
   (barracuda fins
      puffs of red dark
        devil teeth gleaming through)
   the end of nothing.
Alien, I!
among the shards of Eden!

Strange Cities

72. BLACK POEM

into the darkest octaves
my child mind creeps
black on black
white becomes
sulfurous gloomy blue-gray
shuddering with the
blows of underworld
iron clapper in
thud-mouth bell
booming breakwalls bell
fascinating horror
vast Gothic bell tower
in the sky
hollow and rage-shaken
black like rotten tooth
laced with age-blackened
ornature that looks
and smells of decay
intricate and sky-abrasing
ragged and rounded like a
festering thigh stump
wave upon wave of
deepening shadow-shaking
rocks the rat-streets
   cold
how cold it must be
in that hollow tooth
that gaping rot skull
brooding black ice cave
how high
       the lonely birds
              and fly well past

73. JUNGLE OPSIS

        **(cautious tread)
     the jungle is alive with the
        timeless patter of a clear,
          sunless stream

patters-
platter
     on green cistern rocks; empt-
              empty echoes...

       **(tiptoes, a wary hand)
       hanging garlands of vine block
            vision.)
       **(timid tread)
    chattering animals wild movement silence petrified
       **(fear)
persistent cry of plumed
beady-eyed marvel
       **(hypnotic ignorance, fear, hatred)

I Run Back
   to the Beach
   to the Sunlight
   to the blinding Sand

     (   )
 At my back, echoes
suddenly explode in the
green halls of wonder!

74. HITCH-HIKE ENDLESS HIGHWAY

I've got an endless highway
crawling on ahead of me
(and who is crawling?)
sometimes lost in fog
    in picture mists
    filled with dreams
sometimes vanishing
when there are no lights
blows right through you
wind of passing trucks
destination from your hands/leaves it in the mud
face-down on its message.
    Someone I know
    once told a joke
    but forgot to laugh:
    "If I want to go somewhere
    I'll have to sell my car."
    we laughed at him,
    but who knows, maybe
    they're happier,
    when I crawl they ride
    when I ride they crawl
I've got an endless highway
crawling on ahead of me
I've got an endless highway
pushing from behind
I must keep going
    can't look back
I thought once
I was charting the universe
    setting guidelights
        on the farthest
            seas ⇨

I was floating in it all
and getting educated
to expand my mind
to contain it all//but
it contains me
    and I saw where it's at
The past is vast
the present is
a passing moment
the future ain't at all
    I'm stuck somewhere
    bouncing between the
   chewing wheels
    of time's nonsense train
somewhere between the wheels of
present and the future,
the wheels of now
        and a lot of
       empty dreams
         until I sigh
          and lie
       down and die
under the wheels as
present becomes
the future.

75. COLD PASS THROUGH ME

Cold passes through me
my pores
stiffen and hum drily
with Aeolean winds
that shake and shatter me
silently

My thoughts rise
like the bloated winter clouds
snow within
nobody knows
only the snow
in the pit of my stomach

No fire burns here
but the cold unconsuming flame
of a vision of Moses
signifying nothing
in the tangled underbrush
of my mind

Lord the birds
a flutter of distant wings
in the clouds
a million million miles away
inside me   ⇨

Cold
your body is like the body
of a woman I had
last night
Only the fire of despair…

…cold
I was drunk
a winter's night
or fall
even summer
to me
I was shaking-cold

In the month of New Ember
A crow came to me
sat on my shoulder and
wept
And there was vastness
between my shoulders
old
wind laden with
the dust inside a
wine barrel those breath
of red & warm & forget
has evaporated
to feed the cold
unconsuming fires
of it all   ⇨

I feel the opiate
opiate of being & being
too dull to know all knowledge
coursing through the ubiquitous
vein-like entrails of
(thoughts)
that hunted, bleeding, gut-spilling sow

I have crossed the river
not knowing whence I came
Now in my 18th year
I stand wet naked cold alone
on the muddy bank
the coin is in my hand
And not even a boatman
all my cherished aspirations
handful of coins
I think I lost them
long ago

What is this land
I have come to
that it should gloom
with the water vapors
of gray sky
and tell me nothing   ⇨

now in the night
the mist has gone
the river has become
a vast ocean or eternity
I see now
a city
the dark banks
extend into nothingness on both sides
the lights of the city
neon foolishness
they twinkle
in the tide heaving slowly at my feet
the dark banks
extend into nothingness on both sides
though I think I can see
the tide that heaves twinkling at my feet
stretched out across the heavens
and in the dark
banks of my mind
wind the cold
blows to me
thoughts
of a perfumed whisper
the comfort
someone passes me
on dark street
amid the banked snow
a pleasant girl   ⇨

streets
lines
a straight line is
the shortest
distance
between two points
between
empty
public squares
or just crossroads
I can wander aimlessly
and nothing
will fill the
emptiness inside me
I can stand under
the lights
I can watch cars
I can watch people
I can
I can stand on the curb
and when the streets
and the spaces at their ends
are empty
there I am
there
are the street lights.

76.   FISH POOL WISDOM

Wisdom
born of
pools of foaming
fish sperm bobbing
on grassy stream surface
in desolate grassland countryside
spit
from the wind
drawn across the sky
(by a boy's moist finger
  in a department store window)
falls
to earth
gray clouds settle in bushes
along a glimmer-cold stream bank
(lazy stream life slow
wallow ponderously nowhere
nowhere just a streak a hiss a
cry of life brief as the flash of a
meteor brief as
a curve in the stream)
gray clouds icy with glitters
in spider-shit clinging
like eroding detergent
in the spread-arm
crucified twigs
dry as bone

a wind
and winter passes
spidershit germinates
busts and crackles
nothing happens   ⇨

nothing
cosmic abortion
death before life
"Now I lay me down to sleep…"
drifts across the empty road
fireside warmth on a
telephone pole
security —
knows nothing of the
parents' quarrel
the needs, the passions,
the fomenting desires
the seething shrill
anguish of the mouthless mind
echoing dully in the
grating, blood-whispering
bone chambers of the head

the trees
blew their minds long ago
they just are
seek an answer from a tree
beat your head against a wall
nothing
nothing
agony of having intellect
agony of wondering
agony of searching the streets
the long-deserted back roads
the cloud-brush-swept skies
searching for an answer
only a mind could ask
what it cannot answer
mind: a leaf
growing inward   ⇨

till it bursts
sprays juice
sprays despair
sprays
what lingers
on a night-air tincted
with the faint poisonous
exhalations of plants

(leaves, trees, even
ugly poisonous
   curling plants
living hidden in the
darkness and stench
of hidden-flowing
   swill rivers)
exhalations of stranger
faint toxic whiff
of methane of jet trail
of crashed burned towed car
of comet trail
of star trail
alien and solemn
     forbidding
as the icy Medusa bush
stripped to its
    crackling branches
and gnarly twigs
struggling
half in half out
of the frozen
   winter-night pond
lair of snakes
anguish of the mind
nightmare of
no awakening just
deepening sleep…

77. DISEASE LYRIC

I woke up at 10 tonight
been sick a long time
an I haven't seen sun
no, only tired dawn
when I go to bed
at breakfast

It's a strange world I
wake into on this schedule

never know ahead
just what it's gonna be

only
some of the faces I saw before
got there too.

78. YMCA

I feel
butchered and quartered
staying at the Y

everything's neat and clean
clichés and christian virtue

somebody took a toothbrush
and cleaned out the bathroom
so it gleamed
he was queer

someone's crawling
in the woodwork
cleaning away
a million stale particles
of long-ago dreams

but he can't get
to the ceiling
because he's not big enough
and there it's all black

yellow buses come and go
shouting kids, on and off
"our heart's in our purpose!"
"our heart's in our purpose!"
this place makes me sick   ⇨

I've got the tower window
at the Y
now I can see everything
I see the drops
before they hit
I see cars
in their narrow lanes
before they crash
but only I know when

I see a crowd in the middle
 of the block
where can they be going
all the different people
why do they stand together
hippies and patriots
when they rip each other apart?

someone asks a cop
looks to the law
but he shrugs
cant help you pal
thirty centsll get you there
somebody snickers
and I think he's a rebel

now the crowd again
         looks blankly
      into oncoming traffic
         (waiting? hungry?)

I've lost every hunger
except the hunger to speak
and then I can only
speak of hunger.

79.   LOST WORLDS

Morning I Set Sail
To the lost rivers
of a forgotten world

   gently my sail
blossomed out purple
  on the morning air
carried me
through mossy arches
deeper and deeper
into a clockless day
through a plain of
ripening corn
through a sky
or airy blue
through canal-street cities
  by the windows of their haunted houses
glitter-fish flashed
as the rivers crossed
and I rocked faster
on a current madly rushing
  between mermaid reefs that waved good-bye
lost among crossing rivers bubbling through the
whisper cities
in the shadows
I could see stars
cotton-cloud
sunshine
easing my mind
tremble-fingered I touched
  the sleep-leaf bank coming to a gentle stop   ⇨

weak-kneed I got out and stood before the
immemorial forest
echoes of trees
touching in the
hollow canyons of deep
like bright-tone bells
I shook my head
and heard the mellow notes
of an ivory flute
whispers of a pale decay
in the sun-drenched leaves
timeless murmur of a brook
as I bent down to drink
      I saw myself sailing softly into
evening castles
of a deeper world
I turned and watched
   my sail crumple
      like a silk kite
         and in its place
grew a vast kaleido
scope balloon
now I was back
inside the boat
wheeling madly on
an anchor chain
and I felt the breeze
of passing stars
blackness caught me up
shook me up and
took me up
in a watermelon sky
full of thousand boats
ballooning softly in a noisy carnival ⇨

of laughing clowns and
happy faces
friends and lovers
gathered here in a
land of cooky stars
rocket witches silvery trails
black cats a hundred
barging far below
on a smoking raft of straw
until I saw
we were in a land
of giants
falling in a golden trumpet
head-over-heels
in the laughing corridor of
the great bells
of a voiceless trumpet
landed on a blade of grass
watched the flow above
tumbling crystals of
rainbow colors
suddenly I was alone with empty night above
sitting in an empty street
crying softly to myself
I was back to size
stumbling in alley-ways
looking for the lost
lost worlds of wonder

80. MOLLUSKS

Mollusks we trillion
weaned out of
the sand of dreams
    hardened by
    sun
    wind
    storm
    rain
    cold
    fire
we creep to the sea
over a beach of groaning woods
        acid sand
        crystal sand
        red sand
leaving ring
    after ring
a tunnel
growing darker
    to the sea
some stop
    don't start again
        crumble
with every storm
    we dig deeper
caught in the first soft lines
soft water soft bubbles we
push on through a millennium
as afternoon sunlight begins to
falter into darkness' first and
most vague intimacies of gray
    In the first waves we
        lose comprehension
    each wave
        a billion years
        lost, snapped, momentary time
        we grow   ⇨

··············tunneling
··············darker
··············ah the sea

we who still move on
outposts ever farther separate
············leave the curling trappers
············in the cities in the green waters
············where they wait brightly to
············share their shells with the
············lover, the warmer, the killer

no
for us
is only the
whale-like sea
vast womb as we travel
··················unravel
······················backward in time
················alone
············into
··········the
········darkening seadeeps

I am the fisherman of the
ages waiting lonely and hidden
eons a million million in the
abysmal canyons of a silent black sea
fading slowly
··················until I crumble
am dragged deeper still alone
by clouded toneless waters

············— Bell of dreams —

81. HYMN TO THE NEW KING

Come let us sail away,
let's fill our sails with wind
toward the morning sun.

Let the briny deeps of the sea
raise white fingers
to carress my ship's bow.

Sing, ye maidens waiting
on the shore, the glories of
Helen, & of your new-found king.

Our fathers' heavy-bearded
faces stare out from the waves
nodding solemn assent...

@@@ Beautiful Planets

82. SAILOR'S RETURN

       calm has returned
truly, sunset draws near
softly the sea
       washes the brine-white bow
of my slack-rigged ship
       and she lists slightly
turns
       straightens
       draws a wondrous, warm taut
    and begins to run happily along the
  shores of never-ending peace
looking for the coves of cool evening.

83. DOG LOVE

BY THE fiery light of my last sun
the day wandered somewhere and
whistle as I might
it never came back
only the dog came back
running slow and sleepy down the
       country road.

84. HOT DOG VENDOR ON THE BEACH

The wealth was in the hot dog vendor's hands:
Timmie   had big round blue eyes
     bought two   ate his
gave one to little Janie who
broke hers
     gave part to   ate hers
     Spotty the dog-
and so there were three.

85. LANDSCAPE, WITH CATS

On moving in; after night emptiness:
to acquire these old friends:
A tomcat named Joseph; cat-like Judith; and
        cat-Rose with her litter of 5:

    c a t s : l a n d s c a p e
    s i l e n t m i n d – f i l l e r s
    i n e m p t y n i g h t r o o m s

        . . . .

--split wood, stacked wood. Built fire-in-place. 1 hr
cleaned kitchen:spices:measuringcups;dishes: <u>2 hrs</u>
                                                      3 hrs

                            = home/love

86. SUMMER THICK AIR

What could go wrong
on a day like this,
when the summer air
is thick and sweet
like a heady wine?

What could go wrong
on a summer day
when the sticky road is squeezed
between massed green leaves
and banks of perfumed dogwoods?

87.   SAND AND SUN

When
a dog ambles across
scathing sand with wagging tail
head bowed before the booming breakers
turning clumsily on four legs to
catch the brilliant sun, full on
a friendly canine face
pale tongue
when old weary legs lie stretched from
a wall worn by sand and wind
feet encased in old black lace-ups
feet tired
and sun makes tired and wine makes tired
and eyes make tired
Sleep
Sleep - grit has lost its teeth
wind is like warm water -
warm
tingling mixture
barking happily

88. ANARCHIST DANCES III

I am sorry.
You have forgotten the Pleasure
so
You must return to the Pain.

As you hang up your houses
and have your cars ripped in half
the EARTH will take your tickets.

89. EVENING

        Ten Thousand Fires
autumn sun crowned grassy woodland
  so very long ago

       and where swallows drowned in
                            evening's spires
  bells sang together in drowsy dusk

not a word was said
        and before long
it was all dark and over.

90. WRITING POEMS/INTROSPECTION

  (Sue)
  at 3 a.m.
  <u>one thinks the strangest things</u>

in 12 hours I will be
sucked into the sky shot over
a cloud dragged through the hills
<u>dropped in New Haven</u>

I am fearful of this new forest
I don't want to look too deep
for fear of the face, the eyes, looking back

tonight I saw the pond
and looked past the glitters
at the sunken worlds
bittenoff ends of mourning dragwillows

I will not go to your castle
because there am I
and because I fear your dungeons
chain and pounding weary mallets

    bottle of blood
    I have prickled my hand
    on a foreboding thorn

oh forest
if you knew

the things I have seen

the cities I have stood and wept in
the transdimensional highways I have hitched
 run through by fast cars
 and barreling truck monsters

91. SEA BED

My bed is my sea-bed.
There I soak-in-green-dessication,
Soaped by butterflies of sunlight.
The sea can be held in a bath tub,
even in a thimble.

In that faint glimmering of consciousness
Sleep is deep as the wordless womb.
Marble tomb flooded by sea water.
--Sending trillion-kilowatt hoarse whispers
to my neighbor Draco Pulsar, *Om*,
says Draco, --*Shanti*, chirps
the echoing basilica with nuns' voices.
The stones answer in voices of stone.

I am I-less. Probed by the
Panicked but dully glad feelers
of my ego-head. "Awake," it says
in a faint, far voice, "awake!"
You owe it to yourself.

It is the voice that writes
Odes addressing the
sea-hanging cliffs.

92. SEA WIND

Making peace with my destiny
I go to the islands.
No more winter this heart
I sun like soap.
You my love, with me
Would have it no other way.
A ship, darling, a ship
Waits at dawn, dewy sails.
Waits at dawn mist-hung
Rocking salty by green stones.
A captain and a sailor there
come to cheer falling sails.
A captain and a sailor there
come to cheer rising seas.
Briney gale whistles eerily
 in the nostrils of my skull,
Howls salty Glorias
while the good-bye boy
      madly shakes
      the ship's bell.
Briney wind rubs our eyeballs
The wind, morning muezzin.
Pre-sun, dim pearls the sea-drops
The wind, rubbing our backs.

93. CHILD: COLOPHON

Come, child, sit by the stove.
Outside the storm may howl,
The rain be cold and sleek
Over the backs of the trees,
But you shall read, read,
and be lost into a brighter world.

www.ingramcontent.com/pod-product-compliance
Lightning Source LLC
Chambersburg PA
CBHW031942070426
42450CB00005BA/344